The Willow Pattern Story

Eugenie Summerfield

Nelson

Once upon a time, long long ago, there lived a rich old Chinaman in a very grand house which stood beside a river where weeping willows grew. All around the house were gardens with flowering fruit trees of all kinds — apple, cherry, orange and peach.

In his house the old Chinaman had the finest things that money could buy. But he was mean and never gave anything away.

Every day he gloated over his treasures, saying, "All these beautiful things are mine! They all belong to me!"

Now, this mean old man had only one
daughter, Koong-see. She was not like her father.
She was as beautiful as the sunrise.

"She is mine," the old Chinaman said, "so no
one shall take her away from me. And no one
shall marry her, unless he is as rich as me."

The old man did not know that Koong-see
already loved Chang, a young man who was not
rich at all. He was the old man's secretary.
Chang was clever and worked hard, but the old
man was furious when he heard that Chang
wanted to marry Koong-see.

4

"I will never let my daughter marry, unless it is to someone as rich as me," he said again and again.

He would not listen to anything Koong-see had to say and, that very day, he ordered that Chang be sent far away. He also told his servants, "A wooden fence must be built around my land without delay. It must close off every footpath. From now on, no one shall come onto my land unless *I* say so."

Koong-see wept and thought to herself, "I shall run away."

But the old man turned to her and said, "You, Koong-see, will stay in the willow-tree house, where you will be guarded night and day. You shall not leave there until I say."

Koong-see pleaded with her father, but it was no use.

"My mind is made up," he declared, "and I have also decided that you shall marry my old friend Ta-jin."

Ta-jin was exceedingly rich but he was also old and fat. So, of course, Koong-see cried more than ever. Her father took no notice of her tears.

"You shall marry Ta-jin in the spring," he said, "when the peach tree is in full bloom."

Poor Koong-see was so unhappy! Day after day she watched sadly from her window as first the golden willow tree burst into bud, then into bloom. Then she watched the buds beginning to form on the peach tree.

She cried softly to herself, "Soon, all too soon, the peach tree buds will open and bloom. Then I must marry that fat old Ta-jin. Oh, Chang! Chang! Please come back and rescue me!"

Then, as she looked out across the water, she saw a tiny shell boat with a paper sail floating towards her. Quickly, before the servant guarding her had seen, Koong-see reached down and took the little shell boat from the water. Inside the little shell was a message from Chang.

"Be brave, dear Koong-see. Be ready soon to escape with me."

Koong-see cried again, only this time they were tears of joy. Although she felt happier than she had for many days, she could not help wondering how Chang would get past her father's guards. But she said to herself, ''He will surely find a way because he is so clever. I must be brave until he comes.''

Now the very next day, fat old Ta-jin arrived.
Everyone noticed him. He was dressed in purple
and gold. He waddled into Koong-see's father's
house with a great army of soldiers and servants,
all laden with presents and precious jewels. But
no one noticed Chang arrive.

9

There were so many people, and so much
hustle and bustle in and around the old
Chinaman's house, that Chang slipped quietly in
amongst the crowd, without being seen. He hid
until it was dark among the trees, close to the
willow-tree house where Koong-see was kept
a prisoner.

That night a great feast was held at the old
Chinaman's house. Whilst Koong-see's father
and Ta-jin were eating and drinking, Chang
crept from the trees. From underneath Koong-
see's window, he called softly to her to come
down, ''Now, Koong-see! Come down
quickly, now!''

Without making a sound, they ran through
the garden to the bridge which would take them
to the other side of the river. But, just as they
reached the bridge, they were seen by one of the
guards. And soon the old Chinaman, Ta-jin and
all his soldiers were chasing after them.

11

"Into the boat, quickly!" Chang whispered.

12

He had a little boat hidden under the willow trees. He and Koong-see jumped together into the boat. Away they sailed right out of reach of the angry shouting men on the wooden bridge. They sailed to an island far away and lived happily for a while, but that is not the end of the story. The evil Ta-jin said, ''They shall not get away from me! I shall go on searching and I shall punish them for tricking me.''

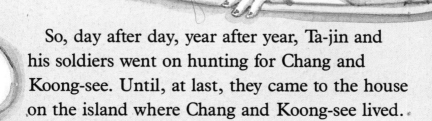

So, day after day, year after year, Ta-jin and his soldiers went on hunting for Chang and Koong-see. Until, at last, they came to the house on the island where Chang and Koong-see lived.

"They will not escape me now," shouted Ta-jin.

He ordered his soldiers to surround the house and set fire to it at once.

"Soon they will come running out, begging for mercy," he said.

He waited and he waited.

No one came from the house, which was soon
burnt to the ground. But then, as the fire and
the smoke died away, from the ashes there rose
up into the sky two white doves, calling softly to
each other,

"C-h-a-n-g! Chang!"

"Koong-see! Koong-see!"

Everyone who heard this story said, "Ah, true
love will never die. Chang and Koong-see
became the two white doves and they will live
for ever more."

And there they are in the willow pattern, to this very day, for everyone to see. If you look very closely at the willow pattern, you will see the whole of this story is there too.